To Alexandra, Carmella and Gemma

Me and My Piano
Part 2

with Fanny Waterman and Marion Harewood

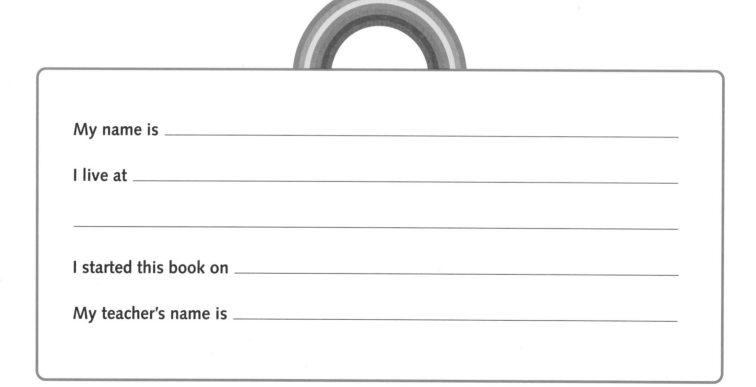

My name is _____

I live at _____

_____

I started this book on _____

My teacher's name is _____

FABER *ff* MUSIC

First published in 1989 by Faber Music Ltd
This edition © 2008 by Faber Music Ltd
Bloomsbury House
74–77 Great Russell Street
London WC1B 3DA
Music setting by Jeanne Roberts
Illustrated by Julia Osorno
Cover design by Lydia Merrills-Ashcroft
Page design by Susan Clarke
Printed in England by Caligraving Ltd
All rights reserved

ISBN10: 0-571-53201-2
EAN13: 978-0-571-53201-8

Hello _____

Here's another piano book with lots of pieces and puzzles for you to enjoy. We should like to introduce you to some new friends – the Zebra, the Crooked Man, the Lady of Niger and her hungry Tiger, the Grasshopper and the Elephant, and many more colourful characters.

Have you seen your own shadow? Footsteps in the snow? Bonfires in the autumn? Moon and stars? You will if you learn to play the pieces in this book. Try to get a star for each lesson. Ten stars deserve a small prize from your teacher or parent!

Have fun!

Fanny Waterman and Marion Harewood

Star chart

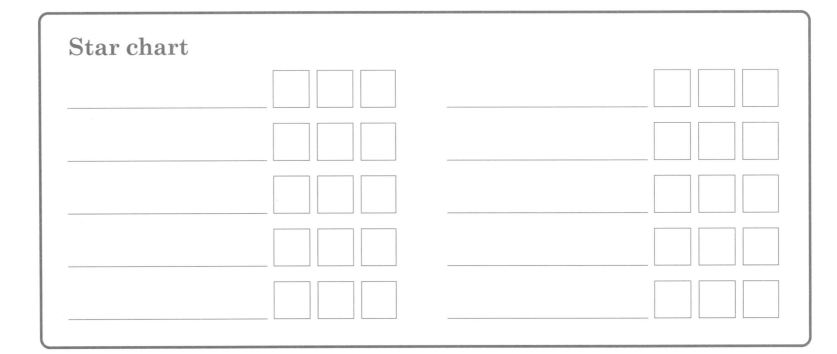

The musical alphabet

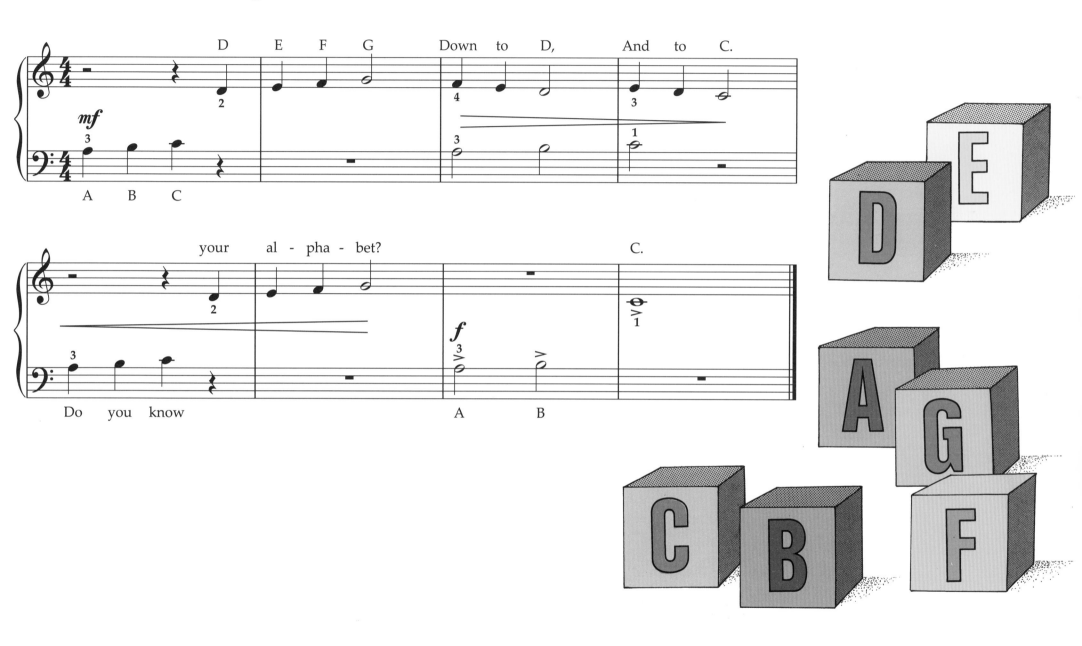

My black cat

p My black cat is ve - ry fat, I give him milk to drink, And

when I ask 'Is that e - nough?' He an - swers with a wink.

The zebra

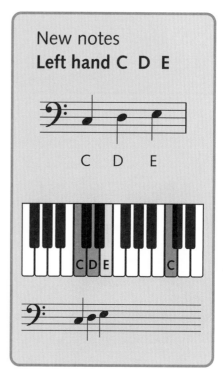

New notes
Left hand C D E

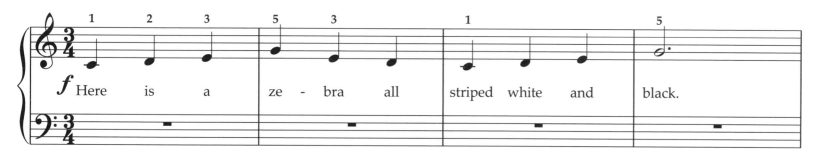

f Here is a ze - bra all striped white and black.

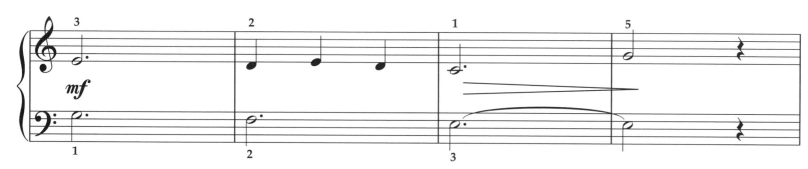

mf

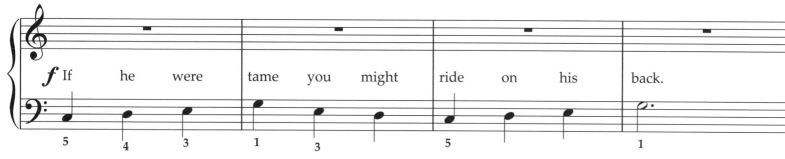

f If he were tame you might ride on his back.

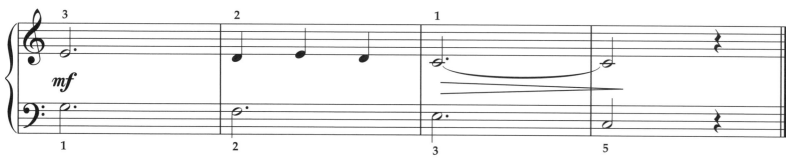

mf

5

New notes LH C, D, E

Notes covered by a **slur** should be played smoothly (**legato**).
Think of them as being under the cover of an umbrella.

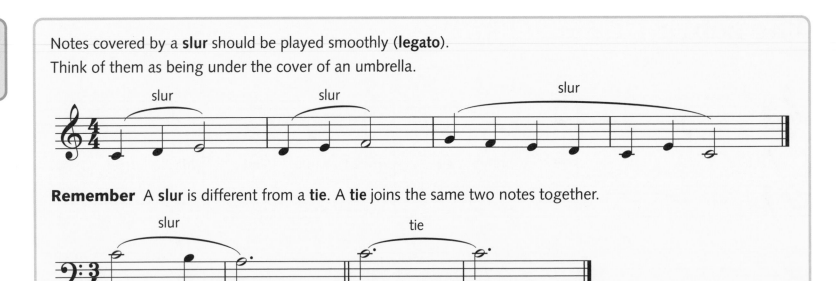

Remember A **slur** is different from a **tie**. A **tie** joins the same two notes together.

Snakes and ladders

There was a crooked man

Footsteps in the snow

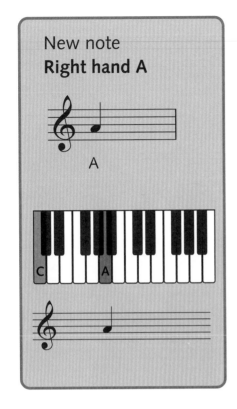

pp = *pianissimo* = **very soft**

8

New note RH A

Twinkle, twinkle, little star

Twin - kle, twin - kle, lit - tle star, How I won - der what you are.

mp

Up a - bove the world so high, Like a dia - mond in the sky,

mf

Twin - kle, twin - kle, lit - tle star, How I won - der what you are.

p

Rain, rain, go away

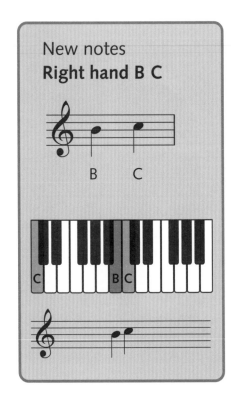

B   C

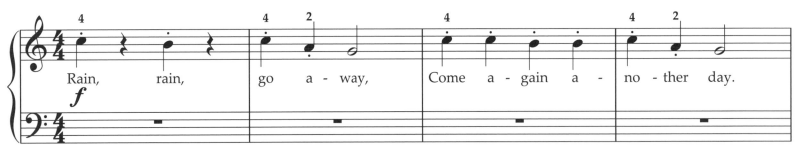

Rain,   rain, | go a - way, | Come a - gain a - | no - ther day.

f

f

Rain,   rain, | go to Spain, | *ff* Ne - ver show your | face a - gain.

ff = *fortissimo* = **very loud**

My shadow

Words by Robert Louis Stevenson

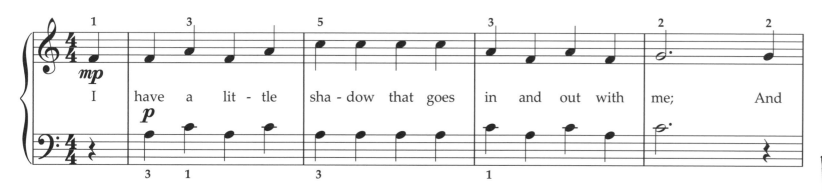

I have a lit - tle sha - dow that goes in and out with me; And

what can be the use of him is more than I can see.

Musical detective

1 Which hand is the shadow, and why?
2 How many Cs does the right hand play?
3 How many Fs does the left hand play?

11

My shadow

New rhythm
Quaver (eighth note)

1 **quaver** looks like this: ♪ or ♪

2 quavers look like this: ♫ or ♫

4 quavers look like this: ♫♫

2 quavers = one crotchet

Remember 1 crotchet = 1 beat

Clap this rhythm, saying the words aloud:

Baa - baa   black   sheep,   have you a - ny wool?

Yes   sir,   yes   sir,   three   bags   full.

One   for the mas - ter and   one   for the dame,

One   for the lit - tle boy who lives   down the lane.

Turkey in the straw

The mouse

Lightly row

$\frac{3}{8}$ means 3 quaver beats in a bar.   A quaver rest looks like this:

Umbrellas

Um - brel - las, um - brel - las go   up   in   the   rain;   And

p   *f*

when   the   sun   shines   they   go   down   a - gain.

p

Some Italian terms (speed)

Andante = **at a walking pace**

Moderato = **at a moderate speed**

Allegretto = **fairly quick, but unhurried**

Allegro = **quick and bright**

When you see this sign ♯ in front of a note, you must play the **black note** immediately above. This sign is called a **sharp**.

Play these **right-hand** notes, naming them aloud:

Now play these **left-hand** notes, naming them aloud:

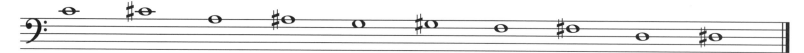

Here's a tune all on **black notes**. Use the third finger of each hand to play alternate notes.

Black key study

When you see this sign at the beginning of a line it means **F** is always **sharp**.
This is called a **key signature**.

To market

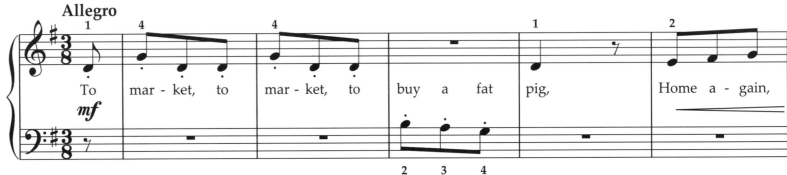

To | mar - ket, to | mar - ket, to | buy a fat | pig, | Home a - gain,

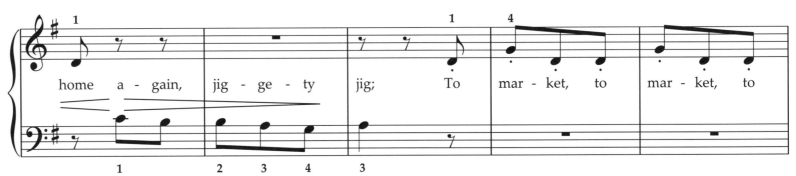

home a - gain, | jig - ge - ty | jig; | To | mar - ket, to | mar - ket, to

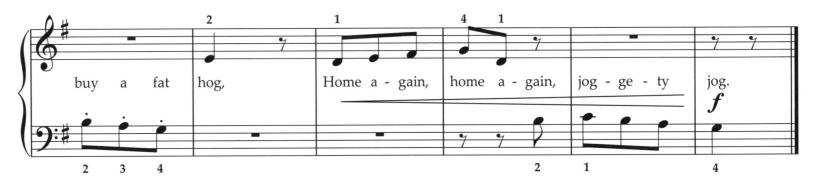

buy a fat | hog, | Home a - gain, | home a - gain, | jog - ge - ty | jog.

Primo = **higher pianist**
Secondo = **lower pianist**

Yankee Doodle *duet*

Later on you can learn
the secondo part.

Monkey puzzles 1

1 Trace over these clefs then copy some more:

2 Name these notes:

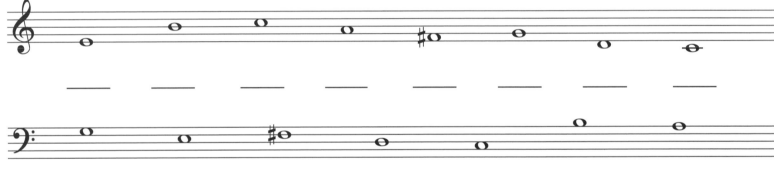

3 Write these notes on the stave:

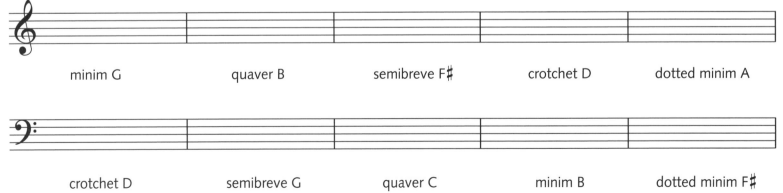

minim G   quaver B   semibreve F♯   crotchet D   dotted minim A

crotchet D   semibreve G   quaver C   minim B   dotted minim F♯

4 How many beats are there in each of these rests?

5 Write the key signature of G major:

6 How many crotchets are there in a dotted minim? _____

How many minims are there in a semibreve? _____

How many quavers are there in a crotchet? _____

How many crotchets are there in a semibreve? _____

♪ = ½ beat = quaver (eighth note)
♩ = 1 beat = crotchet (quarter note)
𝅗𝅥 = 2 beats = minim (half note)
𝅗𝅥. = 3 beats = dotted minim (dotted half note)
o = 4 beats = semibreve (whole note)

7 Add the barlines to these two tunes:

Flats
♭

When you see this sign ♭ in front of a note, you must play the **black note** immediately below.
This is called a **flat**.

J'ai du bon tabac *duet*

Secondo

Old French

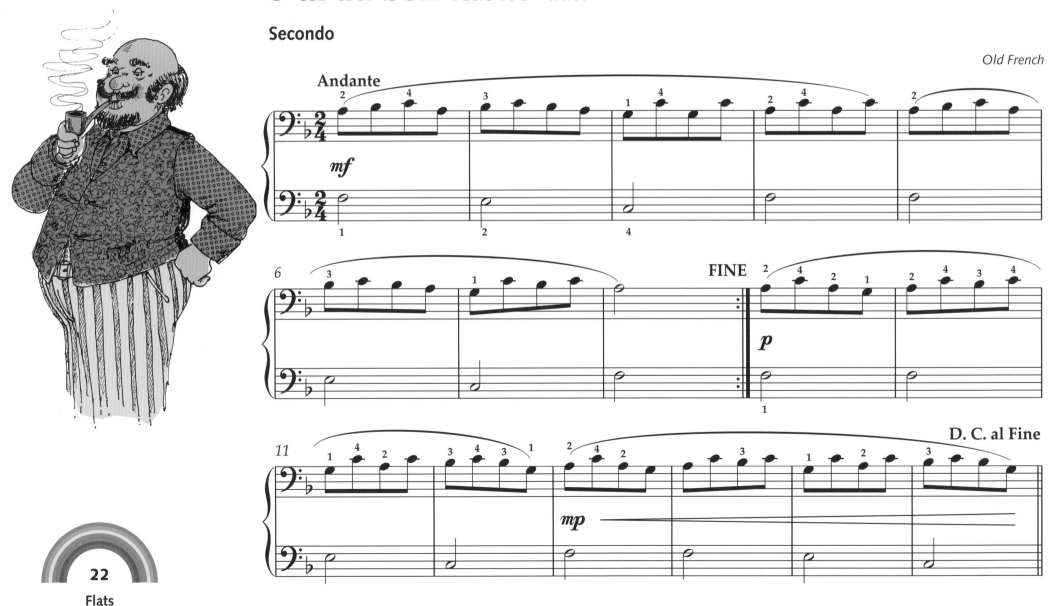

New key
F major

This is the key signature of **F major**.
It means **B** is always **flat**.

J'ai du bon tabac *duet*

Play both hands one octave higher.

Primo

Old French

D.C. al fine
Go back to the beginning and play until you reach **Fine** (the end).

23

New key F major

William Tell Overture

Rossini

DAME FANNY WATERMAN

is a living legend in the world of music, a teacher of international renown, a respected clinician and adjudicator and author of over 30 piano teacher books. As one of the most outstanding and sought-after piano teachers of our time, Dame Fanny Waterman's pupils have won prizes at local, national and international piano competitions, including the Rubinstein and Van Cliburn. Her extraordinary success stems from her concentration on security of technique, whilst instilling a sense of excitement in her pupils by working with their imaginative abilities right from the start.

Dame Fanny Waterman
Piano Treasury Volumes 1 & 2

Two unmissable collections of piano repertoire for intermediate to advanced players, especially selected and edited by the renowned Dame Fanny Waterman. Ideal for performance in competitions, school concerts and as encores, all the pieces have been popular with the great pianists, including Rubinstein and Horowitz. Each piece has been carefully chosen by Dame Fanny for its charm, musicality and educational value and comes complete with her own teaching notes and insights. There are two collections: Volume 1 is for approximately Grade 5 to 7 level and Volume 2 for Grade 6 to 8 level.

> **These Piano Treasury volumes contain my own interpretative insights on all the pieces, reflecting many years' teaching and performing experience. I hope that this collection and my thoughts of a lifetime will help to inspire players: remember there is no age at which we stop learning.**
> Dame Fanny Waterman

> **I do believe that every piano lesson should have a musical injection so the forthcoming practice reflects the interpretation worked on and stimulated by the teacher.**
> Dame Fanny Waterman

On Piano Teaching and Performing

This fascinating insight into Dame Fanny Waterman's teaching approach and the fundamentals of playing technique and musicianship is a must for all pianists. The book distils the knowledge and experience of a legendary teaching career and is packed with inspiring thoughts and advice.

> **This book ... embodies in concise and direct language the most important points of piano playing and of music making ...**
> Murray Perahia

Me and My Piano

Me and My Piano is the best-selling series by distinguished author Dame Fanny Waterman. Designed especially for the needs of the younger beginner and delightfully illustrated throughout, the series aims to make learning the piano an enjoyable experience for both pupil and teacher from the very first lesson. The series consists of seven books, which together provide solid technical and musical foundations for young pianists.

Parts 1 and 2 take the young beginner step-by-step through the earliest stages of piano technique. Amusing rhymes accompanying the pieces encourage and support the learning of rhythm.

Repertoire is a delightful book of first repertoire pieces, which builds on the solid technical and musical foundations established in Parts 1 and 2.

Duets books 1 and 2 provide easy, attractive duets for the young beginner. Designed to complement the progression of Parts 1 and 2, these books feature equal duet parts throughout so pupils can play together. Fun extra material to consolidate learning.

Superscales is a refreshingly different introduction to piano scales for younger players, suitable for use alongside Part 2.

Animal Magic contains essential daily exercises, ideal for developing piano technique in the young player. This book will transform dull practice routines into amusing daily sessions!

Monkey Puzzles

These sets of individual theory papers are perfect for the young beginner, providing lively games and puzzles that will hold the player's interest and make learning fun, whilst helping the teacher cover the rudiments of music in lessons.

The papers cover all aspects of basic theory including time signatures, rests, sharpened and flattened notes, clefs and note duration. The games aid memory and encourage children to think about what they are learning in the context of play. Although designed as a part of the *Me And My Piano* series, **Monkey Puzzles** are ideal for any young musician beginning to study music theory.

The Waterman/Harewood Piano series

The Watermann/Harewood Piano series, devised jointly by the world famous piano teacher **Dame Fanny Waterman** and her co-founder of the Leeds International Piano Competition, **Marion Harewood** provides a wealth of excellent music for the older beginner and a selection of repertoire which is also ideal for adult players.

The series represents a distillation of the thoroughness, inspiration and sense of adventure that characterises Dame Fanny Waterman's own teaching methods. The excellence of the musical material and attractive presentation of the books have won universal acclaim, and the series is established as one of the foremost modern piano methods.

Piano Lessons

These three volumes are the central course books of this highly successful piano method aimed at the older beginner. Technical material is skilfully and imaginatively presented from the very first lesson, while each chapter guides the young player towards the successful performance of a comprehensive selection of pieces and studies.

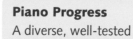

Piano Progress

A diverse, well-tested repertoire of simple pieces by master composers from Bach to Bartók, plus two parallel collections of studies designed to consolidate young players' technique. These volumes span the technical levels of *Piano Lessons Book 1* to early *Book 2*.

The Young Pianist's Repertoire

Each of these books contains 30 or so original pieces, ranging from Baroque to the 20th century. These excellent collections are ideal for intermediate pianists, and can be used alongside *Piano Lessons Books 2* and *3*.

Recital Repertoire

Two valuable introductions to the major piano classics, with 28 substantial repertory works in Book 1 and seven complete classical sonatinas and sonatas in Book 2, with discreet interpretative guidance. To be used alongside *Piano Lessons Book 3* and beyond.

Christmas Carol Time

Twelve really easy piano solos with optional duet accompaniments.

Merry Christmas Carols

Twenty of the best-loved carols and Christmas songs. Stylish yet easy arrangements for solo piano, complete with all the words. This book is also ideal for use in schools.

Nursery Rhyme Time

An irresistible collection of 31 best-loved nursery rhymes, skilfully arranged for the young pianist by Dame Fanny Waterman. The book is attractively illustrated throughout with line drawings designed to be coloured in. Children will have great fun learning as they play.

The Waterman/Harewood Piano series

	Young Beginner		Older Beginner	Intermediate	Advanced
Tutors	Me and My Piano 1	Me and My Piano 2	Piano Lessons 1	Piano Lessons 2	Piano Lessons 3
Repertoire	Me and My Piano Repertoire		Piano Progress 1		
		Me and My Piano Duets 1		Piano Progress 2	
			Me and My Piano Duets 2	Piano for Pleasure 1	Piano Treasury Volume 1
				Piano for Pleasure 2	Piano Treasury Volume 2
			Young Pianist's Repertoire 1		
				Young Pianist's Repertoire 2	
			Two at the Piano (piano duet)		Recital Repertoire 1
	Piano Playtime 1		Piano Playtime 2		Recital Repertoire 2
Exercises	Me and My Piano Superscales				
	Me and my Piano Animal Magic				
Studies	Piano Playtime Studies				
			Piano Progress Studies 1	Piano Progress Studies 2	
Theory	Monkey Puzzles 1	Monkey Puzzles 2			
Miscellaneous	Nursery Rhyme Time				
	Christmas Carol Time				
			Merry Christmas Carols		

Piano Treasury
0-571-53716-2	Dame Fanny Waterman Piano Treasury: Vol.1	£9.99
0-571-53717-0	Dame Fanny Waterman Piano Treasury: Vol.2	£9.99

Me and My Piano
0-571-53200-4	Me and My Piano: Part 1	£5.99
0-571-53201-2	Me and My Piano: Part 2	£5.99
0-571-53202-0	Me and My Piano: Repertoire	£5.99
0-571-53203-9	Me and My Piano: Duets Book 1	£5.99
0-571-53204-7	Me and My Piano: Duets Book 2	£5.99
0-571-53205-5	Me and My Piano: Superscales	£5.99
0-571-53206-3	Me and My Piano: Animal Magic	£5.99

Theory
0-571-51141-4	Monkey Puzzles: Set 1	£6.99
0-571-51142-2	Monkey Puzzles: Set 2	£6.99

Piano Playtime
0-571-50963-0	Piano Playtime Studies	£6.50
0-571-50545-7	Piano Playtime: Book 1	£6.50
0-571-50552-X	Piano Playtime: Book 2	£6.50

Piano Progress and Piano for Pleasure
0-571-50961-4	Piano Progress Studies: Book 1	£6.50
0-571-50962-2	Piano Progress Studies: Book 2	£6.50
0-571-50860-X	Piano Progress: Book 1	£6.50
0-571-50861-8	Piano Progress: Book 2	£6.50
0-571-51023-X	Piano for Pleasure: Book 1	£6.50
0-571-51024-8	Piano for Pleasure: Book 2	£6.50

Piano Lessons
0-571-50024-2	Piano Lessons: Book 1	£6.50
0-571-50211-3	Piano Lessons: Book 2	£6.50
0-571-50311-X	Piano Lessons: Book 3	£6.50
0-571-50636-4	Recital Repertoire: Book 1	£6.50
0-571-50656-9	Recital Repertoire: Book 2	£6.99
0-571-50210-5	Young Pianist's Repertoire: Book 1	£6.50
0-571-50366-7	Young Pianist's Repertoire: Book 2	£6.99
0-571-50232-6	Two at the Piano (piano duet)	£6.50
0-571-50986-X	Nursery Rhyme Time (piano)	£5.99
0-571-50956-8	Christmas Carol Time (piano)	£5.99
0-571-50960-6	Merry Christmas Carols (piano)	£5.99
0-571-52519-9	On Piano Teaching and Performing	£6.99

Contact us
Faber Music Ltd
Burnt Mill
Elizabeth Way
Harlow
Essex
CM20 2HX

t +44 (0)1279 828982
f +44 (0)1279 828983
e sales@fabermusic.com
w www.fabermusicstore.com

@fabermusic
facebook.com/fabermusic

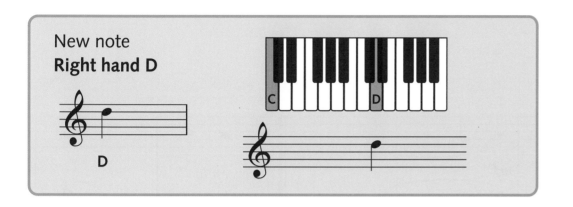

New note
Right hand D

D

Two notes slurred together like this are called a **couplet**.

Drop down on the first note, and spring up lightly on the second.

Post-horn galop

Allegro

Musical detective

1 How many couplets are there?
2 Does the piece get louder or softer?
3 How many bars have repeated notes only?

25

New note RH D

Cuckoo

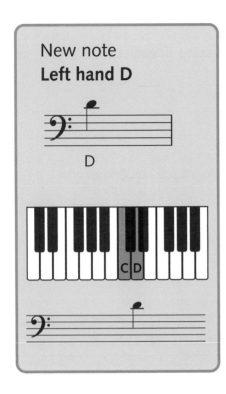

D

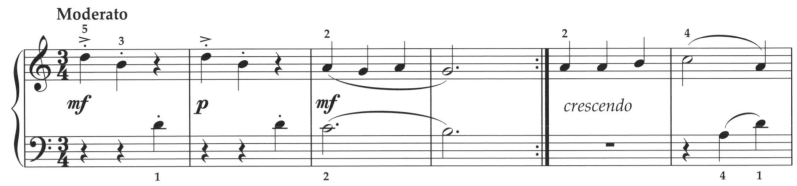

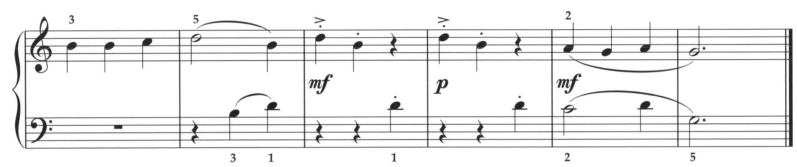

Musical detective

How many times can you hear the cuckoo?

Happy birthday *duet*

Fill in your name in bar 6.

Primo

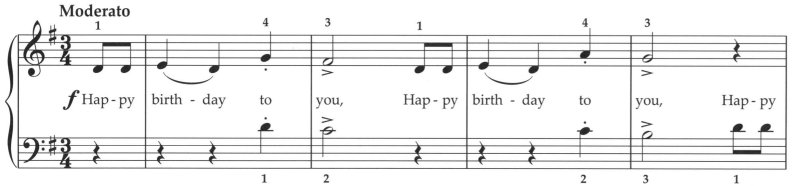

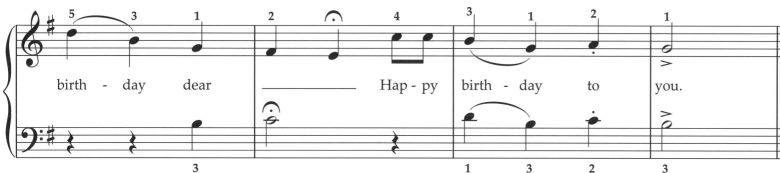

Secondo

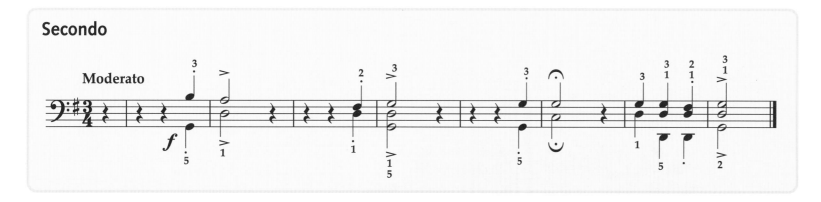

27

Happy birthday

Katie's waltz *duet*

Secondo

Sim. (simile) = **continue playing in the same way**

28
Katie's waltz

Katie's waltz *duet*

Play both hands one octave higher.

Primo

Allegretto grazioso

Grazioso = **gracefully**

29

Katie's waltz

New rhythm
**Dotted crotchet
(dotted quarter note)**

♩.

♩. = dotted crotchet = ♩ + ♪

Bonfire night

Con brio = **brightly**

Con brio

Ro - ckets and | Cath - 'rine Wheels, | Spark - lers and | Jump - ing Jacks | Light up the

sky, What a | glo - ri - ous | sight! | Sand - wich - es, | sau - sa - ges,

Hot dogs and | crun - chy sticks | Make such a | feast on a | cold win - ter's | night.

Bobby Shaftoe

Allegretto

mf Bob - by Shaf - toe's gone to sea___ Sil - ver bu - ckles on his knee,___

He'll come back and mar - ry me,___ Bon - ny Bob - by Shaf - toe.

Bob - by Shaf - toe's bright and fair, Comb - ing down his yel - low hair,

He's my love for ev - er mair, Bon - ny Bob - by Shaf - toe.

Naturals

This sign ♮ is called a **natural**, and it cancels a sharp or a flat.

Sharps, **flats** and **naturals** not in the key signature are called **accidentals**.

This rhythm ➡

sounds like this: ➡

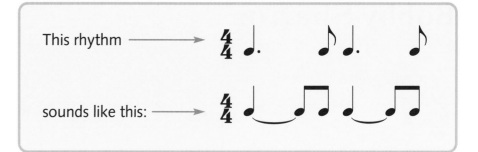

The muffin man

Clap the rhythm of the right hand before you play.

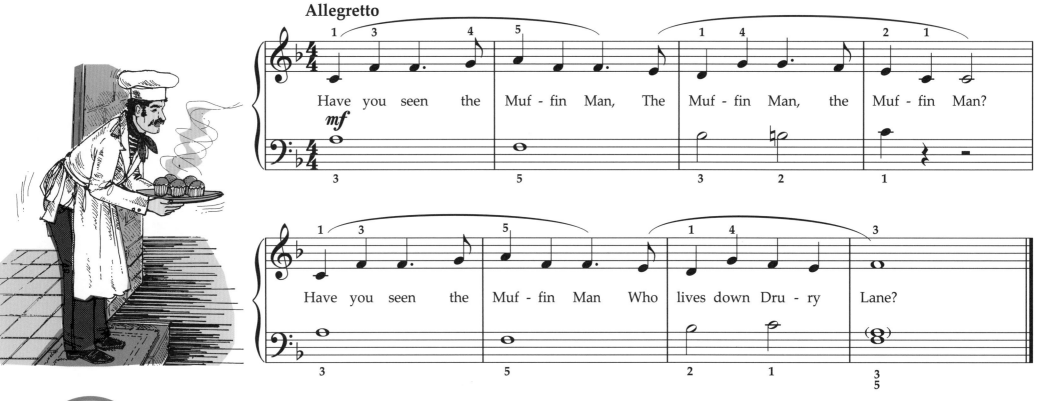

Allegretto

Have you seen the Muf - fin Man, The Muf - fin Man, the Muf - fin Man?

Have you seen the Muf - fin Man Who lives down Dru - ry Lane?

Rock-a-bye baby

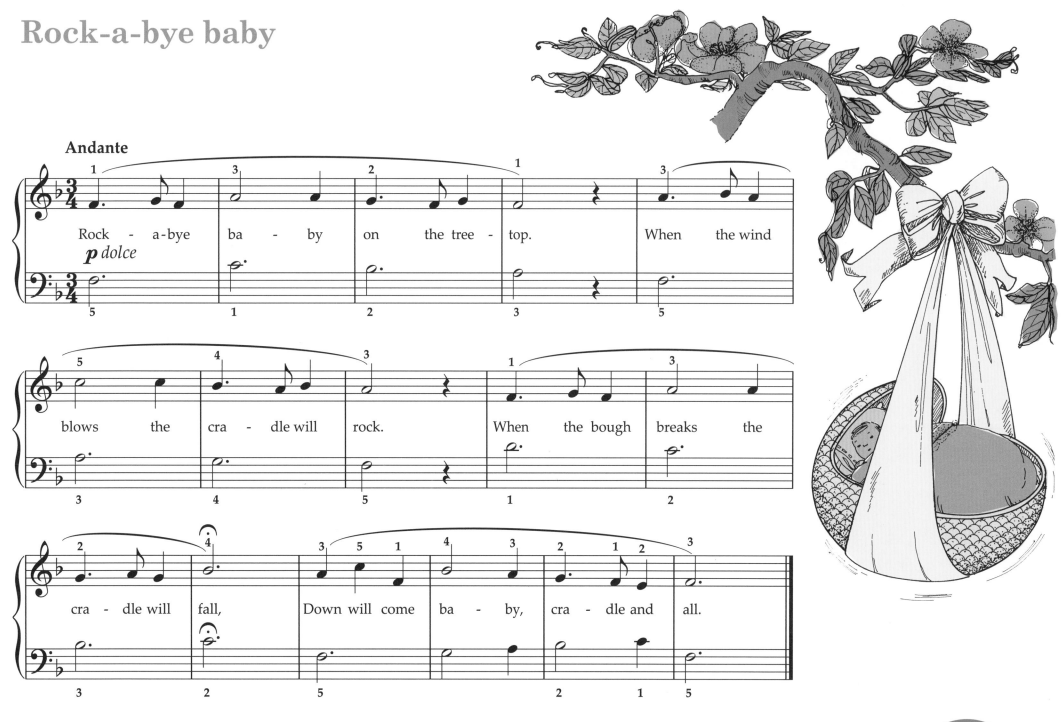

Andante

Rock - a-bye ba - by on the tree - top. When the wind

blows the cra - dle will rock. When the bough breaks the

cra - dle will fall, Down will come ba - by, cra - dle and all.

Dolce = **softly and sweetly**

33

Rock-a-bye baby

Monkey puzzles 2

1 Write these notes:

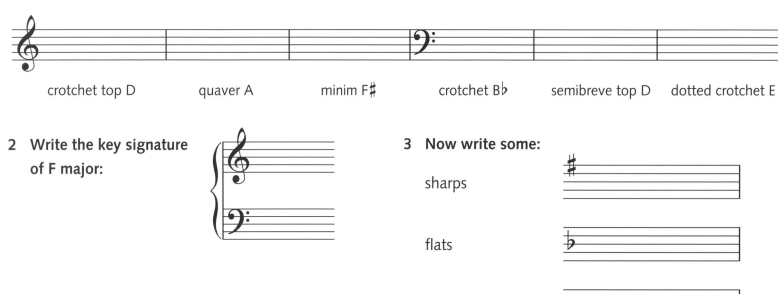

crotchet top D   quaver A   minim F♯   crotchet B♭   semibreve top D   dotted crotchet E

2 Write the key signature of F major:

3 Now write some:

sharps

flats

naturals

4 Mark the B♭s in this piece:

Deck   the   hall   with   boughs   of   hol - ly,   Fa   la   la   la   la,   la   la   la   la

5 Finger these pieces. Do you recognise the tunes?

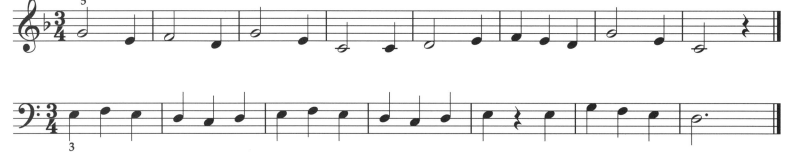

6 Use the music notes to write in the missing letters to make these sentences:

Mozart's ___ ___ ___ taught him to pl___y musi___ ___t ___n

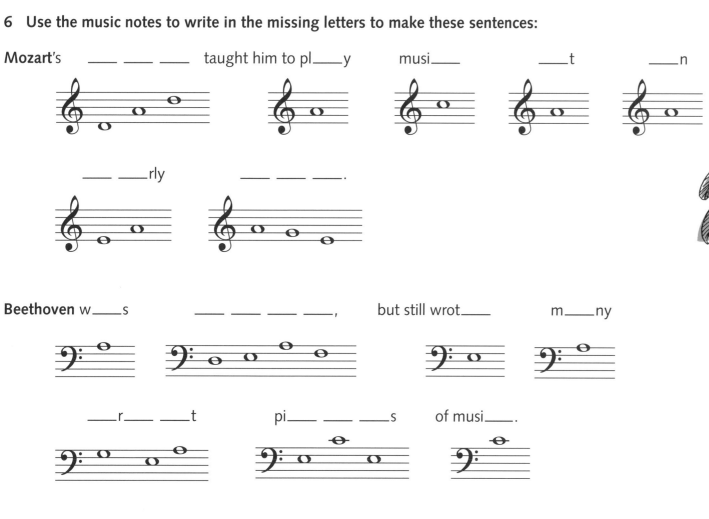

___ ___rly ___ ___ ___.

Beethoven w___s ___ ___ ___ ___, but still wrot___ m___ny

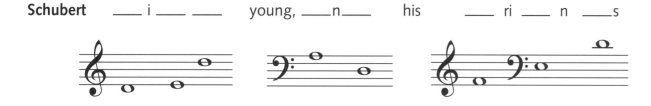

___r___ ___t pi___ ___s of musi___.

Schubert ___i___ ___ young, ___n___ his ___ri___n___s

w___r___ v___ry s___ ___.

Intervals

An **interval** is the distance between two notes.

Play these intervals:

Second   third   fourth   fifth   sixth   seventh   octave

Chopsticks

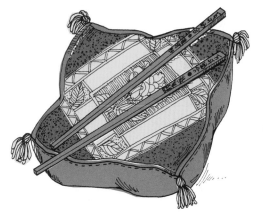

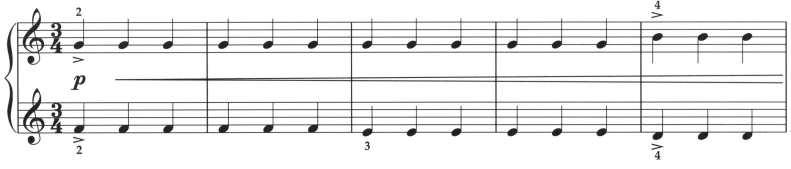

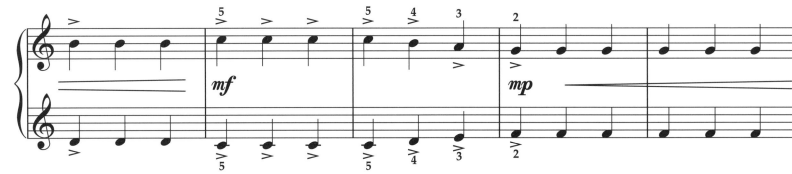

Musical detective

How many different intervals can you find in this piece?

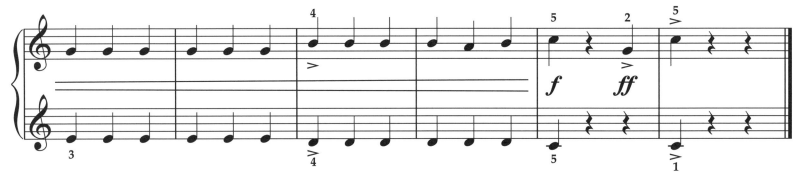

Chords

Two or more notes played together make a **chord**.

Footsteps coming:

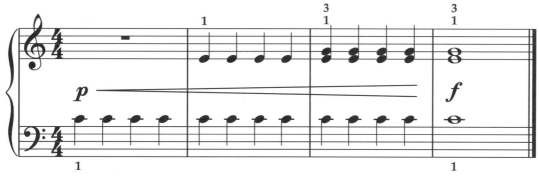

Footsteps going:

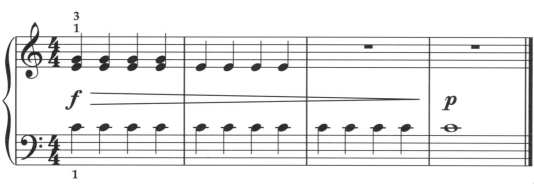

Footsteps coming and going:

Remember: pp — p — mp — mf — ff — mf — mp — p — pp

War drums

Moon and stars waltz

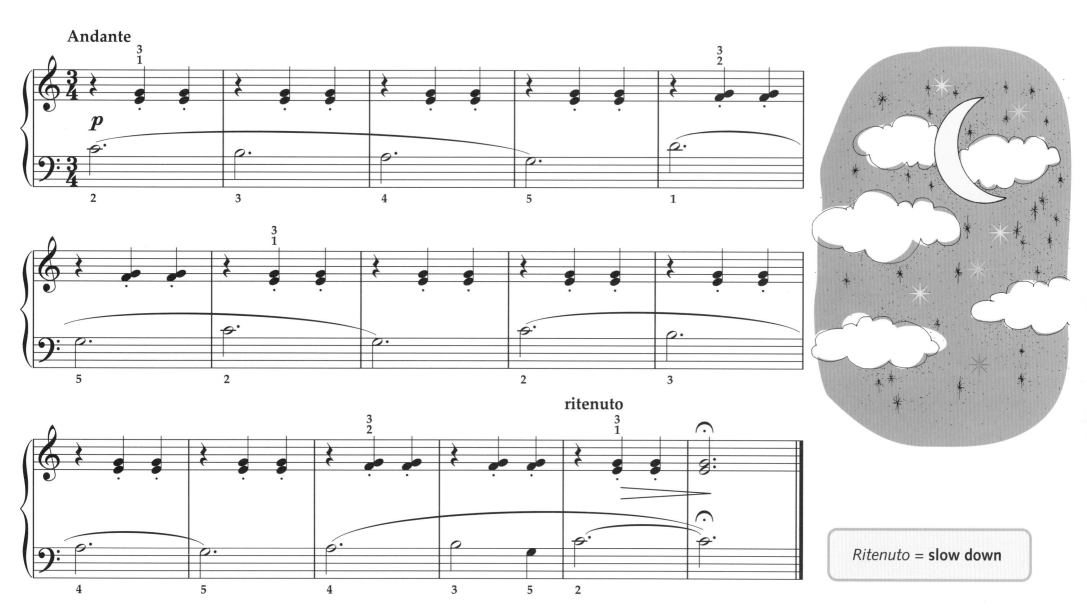

Ritenuto = **slow down**

Musical detective

1 The moon is gliding in the sky and the stars are sparkling. Which hand is the moon and which is the stars?

2 Name the intervals in the right hand chords.

39

Moon and stars waltz

The fairground

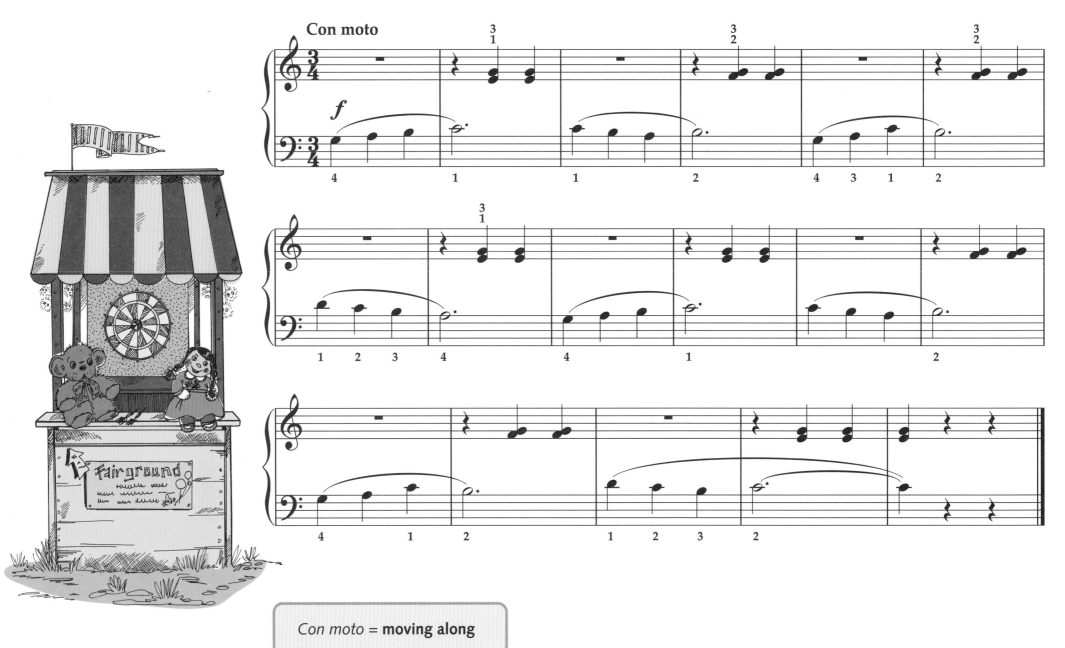

Con moto = **moving along**

Can can

Offenbach

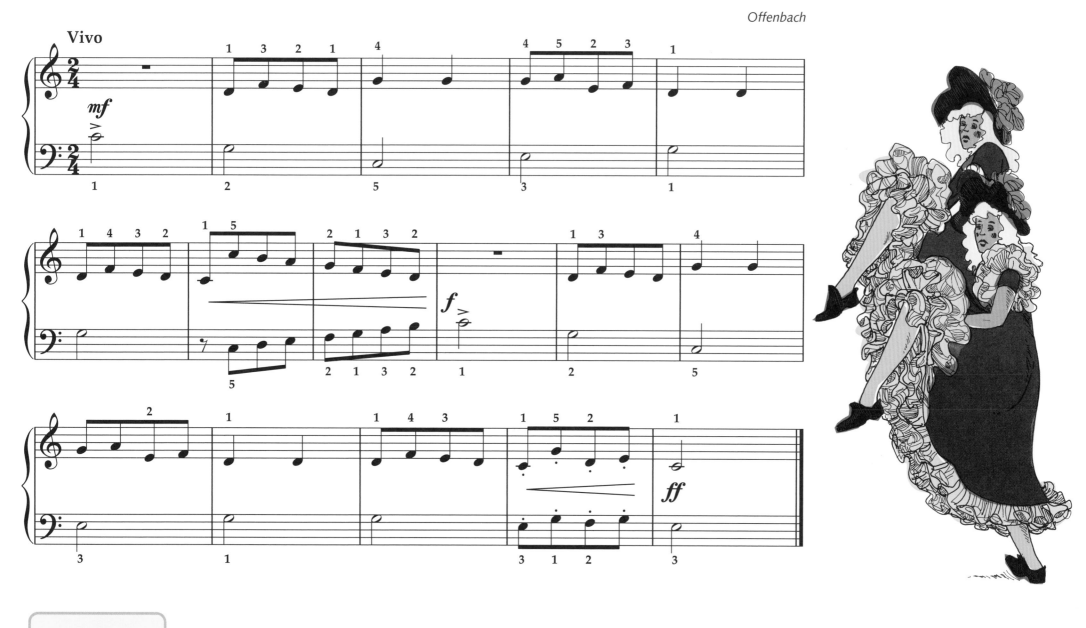

Vivo = **lively**

I'm a little teapot

Three blind mice

New notes LH G, A, B

There was a young lady from Niger

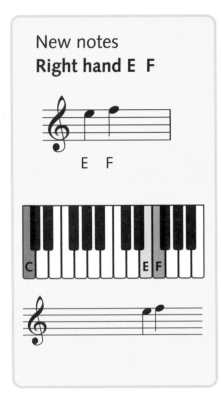

E F

C E F

Allegretto

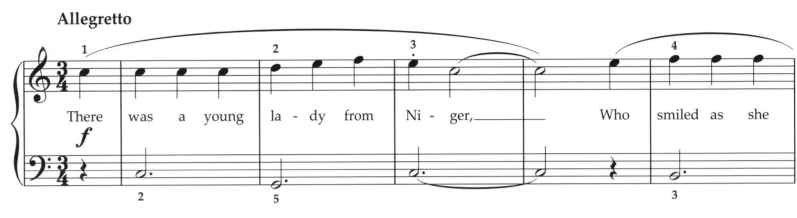

There was a young la - dy from Ni - ger,_____ Who smiled as she

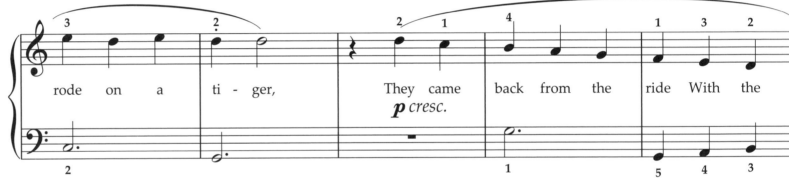

rode on a ti - ger, They came back from the ride With the

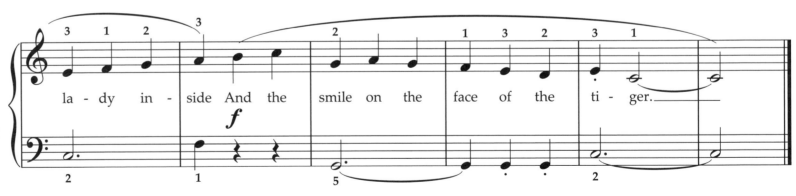

la - dy in - side And the smile on the face of the ti - ger._____

44

New notes RH E, F

The musical ladder

All the notes you have learnt:

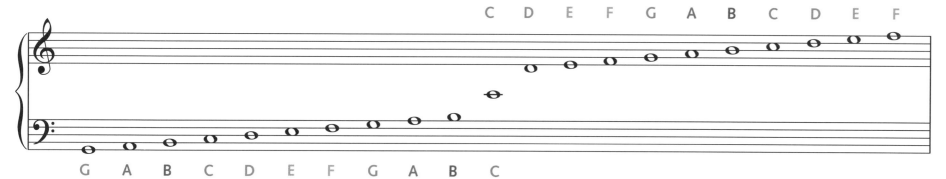

Lines

Treble clef

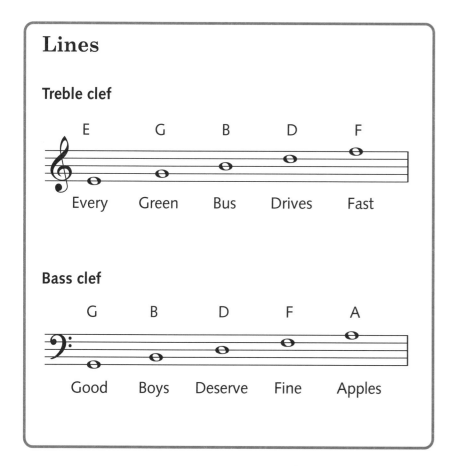

Every Green Bus Drives Fast

Bass clef

Good Boys Deserve Fine Apples

Spaces

Treble clef

F A C E

Bass clef

All Cows Eat Grass

The grasshopper and the elephant

Bucalossi

Leggiero = **lightly**

Musical detective

This piece has lots of accidentals. Put a pencil cross over all the ones you can find.

God save the Queen

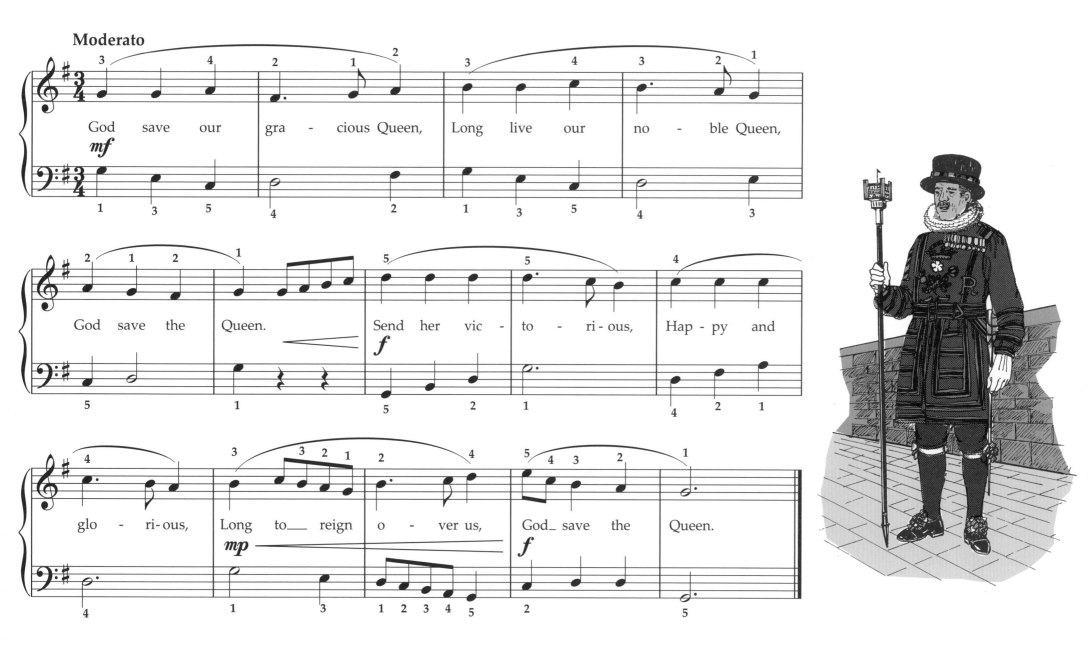

God save the Queen

Rainbow certificate

This is to certify that

_____

successfully completed

Me and My Piano Part 2

on _____

Congratulations!

Fanny Waterman.

Fanny Waterman

Marion Harewood

Marion Harewood

_____

Teacher's signature